MATHEMATICAL MIND

THE UNLIMITED POWER OF THE HUMAN MIND...

JIM KAROL

Copyright © 2025 Jim Karol
All rights reserved
First Edition

Virtual Alliance Publishing
Kirkland, WA

Visit our website at www.jimkarol.com

ISBN 978-1-7345009-1-2 (Paperback)

Printed in the United States of America

Come along on a journey

into one of the world's most FASCINATING MINDS!
Imagine being able to walk into a room full of total strangers
and know things about them,
almost as if you can read their thoughts!
Imagine being able to look into someone's eyes
and being able to know
if they are lying or telling the truth!
What if every day, your brain kept getting stronger
and so powerful that you began to do things,
that you once thought impossible!

Welcome to the world of Jim Karol...

MATHEMATICAL MIND

THE UNLIMITED POWER OF THE HUMAN MIND…

A Cool, Fun way to improve your Math, Memory and Mental skills

"I PERSONALLY DO THESE BRAIN EXERCISES AND GAMES EVERY DAY,

TO HELP BOOST MY

FOCUS, MEMORY AND MOOD"

JIM KAROL

INTRODUCTION

Jim Karol's new book, Mathematical Mind, helps enhance Cognitive abilities, such as Memory, Focus and Attention.

Jim has found that it is possible to improve Memory, enhance Focus and sharpen your Mind, **at any age.**

He has demonstrated that the side effects of aging are not inevitable and it is possible to slow down the effects of aging and grow your brain well into your 70's and 80's.

A former steel worker who struggled with some health issues, Karol developed a method which transformed his own life. Now he is physically healthier than ever and world renowned for his unparalleled memory and mental abilities.

His incredible feats of the Mind and Memory have been featured on The Tonight Show, The Ellen Show, The Today Show and Howard Stern. Jim has toured military bases around the world with the USO and has a true passion and infinite desire to demonstrate his skills and help others.

*"I call Jim the **Holy Grail of Memory.** His work with executives, leaders, staff and students has made a huge difference in the results they achieve in their business and personal lives."*

Tony Dottino, Founder USA Memory Championships

IN THIS BOOK, JIM WILL DEMONSTRATE THE TECHNIQUES AND SIMPLE GAMES HE HAS PERSONALLY USED OVER THE YEARS THAT HELPED HIM TAP INTO THE UNLIMITED POWER OF THE HUMAN MIND...

Steelworker to National Entertainer

I've had a very interesting journey, and this book is my way of sharing some of the lessons I have learned.

I grew up in Allentown, Pennsylvania, and after high school I attended Community College. I didn't do well in college, I spent most of my time in the dining hall playing cards, playing chess, and showing card tricks. Afterwards, I ended up working at the local steel mill.

A lot of stuff happened during that time period that changed my life dramatically. I got married, we had our first child and I met some very interesting people.

After about three months working at the steel mill, I was introduced to a fellow steelworker who loved magic and also owned a magic shop in Allentown.

One day he invited me to visit his magic shop, and that opened my mind to a wondrous new world.

About a week or two later, I met the most inspirational performer of my life. He was an 80 year old sideshow performer at the Allentown Fair known as the Mighty Atom. At 5 feet 4 inches tall, weighing in at 140 pounds, Atom stood in front of the crowd and took out a 60 - penny nail (6 inch spike) and proceeded to bend it in his bare hands.

Experiencing this three minute demonstration by this 80 year old marvel, left such an impact on me, that it changed my life forever. Sure enough, after seeing the Mighty Atom, I just had to know HOW he performed that amazing feat of strength.

After numerous unsuccessful and painful attempts, I was about to give up. However, I decided to give it one last try. Concentrating every ounce of mental energy, I was so focused that the thought of not bending the nail never even entered my mind. Suddenly, in an instant, the nail was bent. It felt fantastic!

This was my first lesson about the unbelievable POWER of the Human Mind and Positive Belief.

The following year the steel mill began massive layoffs. Just like in the Billy Joel song "Allentown", many residents lost their jobs, including me.

With a small child at home and another due any day, I tried desperately to find work, but nothing was available. Without any job prospects, I took my wife's Avon account and went door-to-door selling Avon. I always livened up my presentations by doing card tricks. I don't know if the women felt sorry for me or liked my card tricks, but I quickly became very popular and successful at selling Avon.

I guess that those few months at the magic shop were already beginning to pay off.

One day one of the Avon reps invited me to do a performance in front of several hundred people and it went over really well. About a week later, I was asked to perform another show and soon began performing for local companies and colleges, bending spikes, throwing playing cards, and performing crazy stunts.

Then in 1990, I got a lucky break.

THE LOTTERY PREDICTION

On November 2, 1990, I had a dream about the winning daily numbers in Pennsylvania's lottery. In the weeks following my dream, I told people at 41 of my shows to play 2-2-2 on the PA Daily Number on December 22nd.

Believe it or not, the numbers amazingly came in!

The average state payout is usually 1.1 million dollars, but on December 22nd, my prediction cost the state of Pennsylvania more than 13 million dollars!

The next day I found myself on the front pages of newspapers across the country.

The Lottery Dream

My eerie dream was about a phone call and a man's voice saying, "Jim, you were right! The PA daily number on December 22 really was 2-2-2!" The dream was so REAL that I felt compelled to share it with my audiences. Shortly after, I was contacted to make appearances on numerous television and radio shows. Things were really looking up and I began performing at hundreds of colleges across the country.

The Rest of the Story

However, the most important part of my story didn't really begin until the age of 50, after finding out that I had developed health problems. I was overweight and out of shape and was not prepared for the diagnosis that I was about to receive. I was told that I had a heart problem. I guess the hundreds of cheese steaks and cheese dogs finally caught up with me. Being on the road all the time and eating a dozen donuts a week didn't help much either.

I went home, and I remember telling my wife Lynn, "That's it." "No more cheese steaks." "No more cheese dogs." I began eating nothing but salads and chicken and started riding an exercise bike every day.

Now riding an exercise bike can become really boring, so to keep from being bored, I began memorizing playing cards while riding my bike, then something amazing happened.

My brain was getting Stronger and Sharper each day and I began memorizing all 52 cards in the deck in less then an hour!

I became so motivated that I soon developed my own system that enabled me to remember the playing cards faster and quicker each day. Eventually the system enabled me to begin memorizing anything I could get my hands on. Digits of Pi, zip codes, countries, capitals and thousands of other facts.

Not only did I improve my physical condition and feel better than ever, my Memory, Focus and Mental Strength were beyond belief.

And the best news of all was, I no longer had that heart problem.

I now believe that Positive Energy and Positive Belief can help overcome almost anything. I also believe that it doesn't matter if you are 8 years old or 88 years old, you can still improve your Memory and quality of Health.

I am now in my 70's, and my brain is stronger than ever before…

On the following pages, I will teach you some of my favorite Mental Math and Memory Systems that I personally do every day to keep myself mentally fit…

Jim Karol

⚡ *Studies show that exercising your brain by memorizing NEW facts and NEW information, helps promote brain growth and a healthier brain.*

Chapter One

Attention and Focus Routines

The following routines have helped me improve ATTENTION and FOCUS.

Letters to Numbers

In this first routine we are going to convert letters to numbers and convert all of the numbers into "single digits."

Each letter of the alphabet will be converted to a single digit number from 0 to 9.

Example:

The letter "A" equals "1",

The letter "B" equals "2",

The letter "C" equals "3", etc.

When you get to the letter "J", it would equal "0" instead of "10" because of the single digit conversion.

"K" would be "1" instead of "11", "L" would be "2" instead of "12", etc.

Refer to the chart on the next page, only concerning yourself with the LAST DIGIT.

Letters to Numbers Chart

A = 1	N = 4
B = 2	O = 5
C = 3	P = 6
D = 4	Q = 7
E = 5	R = 8
F = 6	S = 9
G = 7	T = 0
H = 8	U = 1
I = 9	V = 2
J = 0	W = 3
K = 1	X = 4
L = 2	Y = 5
M = 3	Z = 6

EXAMPLES:

The word **CAT**, would be: **3-1-0**

"C" is the 3rd letter of the alphabet
"A" is the first letter of the alphabet
"T" is the 20th letter of the alphabet

(Don't forget, "T" would equal "0" instead of "20")

The word **HAT** would be:
8-1-0

The word **STOP** would be:
9-0-5-6

The word **FOCUS** would be:
6-5-3-1-9

EXERCISE

Make a list of 10 words and convert all of the letters to numbers.

Doing this every day greatly improves my FOCUS. It also plays a huge impact on helping me make split - second and strategic decisions.

The more time that you devote to this exercise the FASTER you will become.

I do this while driving, looking at street names, signs and billboards, converting all of the letters to numbers.

Cool Math Fun

Cool Math and Memory tricks to have fun with your friends

Retirement 65

Put the numbers 1 to 25 in 5 rows of 5 as seen below:

```
 1  2  3  4  5
 6  7  8  9 10
11 12 13 14 15
16 17 18 19 20
21 22 23 24 25
```

Circle any number and cross out the rest of the numbers in the row (Both vertically and horizontally)

Example:

If "7" is selected first, cross out the 6, 8, 9 and 10 horizontally and the 2, 12, 17 and 22 vertically.

Do this 5 times.

The 5 circled numbers will add up to 65, both vertically and horizontally, every time you do it…

Mysterious Number 9

Have someone write down any 3 or 4 digit number.
Have them then multiply that number by 18.
Next, have them CIRCLE any digit in their answer, other than a ZERO.
Finally, have them READ OFF all the digits in their answer, EXCEPT for the one they CIRCLED.
You will INSTANTLY know the CIRCLED NUMBER

Here's How

As they READ OFF the numbers that they circled, simply ADD THE DIGITS in your head.
Next, SUBTRACT the TOTAL from the next highest multiple of 9.

Example:

There 3 digit number is 234
They multiply by 18
The total = 4212
They circled a 4
They read of the digits 2, 1, 2.
You ADD THEM in your head
(2 + 1 + 2) = "5"
Then subtract "5" from the next highest multiple of "9", which in this case IS NINE.
9 - 5 = 4
Your Total is "4", which is the number they originally circled.

FIVE CHADS

"The most Amazing Math Card routine you'll EVER DO"

Hand someone a deck of cards and ask them to CUT THE DECK and complete the cut and you will instantly know the TOP CARD!

How it's done:

For this routine to work, you must secretly prepare the deck ahead of time.

> **The VALUES of the cards are as follows:**
> **ACES are 1**
> **JACKS are 11**
> **QUEENS are 12**
> **KINGS are 13**

(2's are 2), (3's are 3), etc. all the way up to (10's are 10).

Pre-arrange the cards ahead of time as follows:

A♠, 6♣, J♥, 3♦, 8♠, K♣, 5♥, 10♦, 2♠, 7♣, Q♥, 4♦
9♠, A♣, 6♥, J♦, 3♠, 8♣, K♥, 5♦, 10♠, 2♣, 7♥, Q♦
4♠, 9♣, A♥, 6♦, J♠, 3♣, 8♥, K♦, 5♠, 10♣, 2♥, 7♦
Q♠, 4♣, 9♥, A♦, 6♠, J♣, 3♥, 8♦, K♠, 5♣, 10♥, 2♦
7♠, Q♣, 4♥, 9♦

This might seem like a lot of work, but TRUST ME, it will be WELL WORTH THE TIME...

Note that each card is exactly "5" apart.

If you add FIVE to the first card the A♠, you will get the 2nd card, the 6♣. Then if you add FIVE to the 6♣, you will get 11 or the JACK.

This continues throughout the entire deck, so **BE SURE THAT YOU DO NOT DISTURB THE ORDER OF THE CARDS**.

When they cut the deck and complete the cut, the order will always stay the same. Just don't allow them to shuffle the cards.

All YOU have to do is add FIVE to the bottom card and you will know their card, EVERY TIME.

The SUITS of the cards are also in order.
 (Clubs, Hearts, Diamonds, Spades)

An easy way to remember Clubs, Hearts, Diamonds, Spades, is to remember the name: Five "CHaDS".

EXAMPLES:

If the bottom card is a CLUB, then their card is a HEART. If the bottom card is a SPADE, then their card would be a CLUB.

If the bottom card is a 2 of hearts, then their card would be a 7 of diamonds.

**SET UP YOUR CARDS AND TRY IT.
YOU'RE GONNA LOVE THIS!**

NIM SIXTEEN

This is one of the COOLEST Math/Brain games that I ever played. I created a craze with thousands of college students over the years and had such a fun time.

16 colored objects are placed on a table.

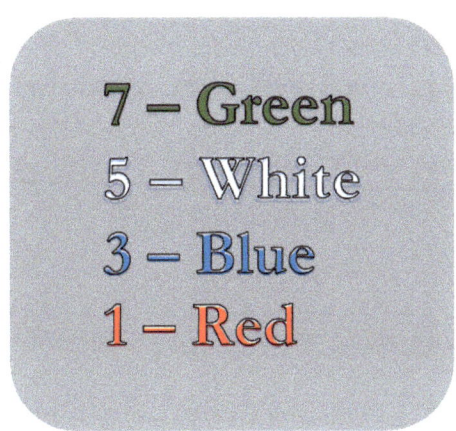

OBJECT OF GAME

YOU and another person alternate turns, removing objects from the table.

Whoever is left with the very LAST object, loses.

💥**The only RULE of the GAME, is:**

YOU CAN ONLY REMOVE OBJECTS THAT ARE THE SAME COLOR...

You can take AS MANY AS YOU LIKE, but you CANNOT TAKE FROM MORE THAN ONE COLOR GROUP AT A TIME...

HOW TO WIN

Whoever takes the LAST CHIP, LOSES!

You must leave certain patterns at the COMPLETION of YOUR TURN:

Here is ONE of the patterns:

After you pick your chips, leave the following pattern:

Pattern of (1,2,3)

EXAMPLE:

(1 Red chip, 2 Blue chips, 3 White chips)

THERE ARE AT LEAST 8 OTHER PATTERNS.

TRY TO FIGURE OUT WHAT THEY ARE AND YOU WILL NEVER LOSE.

💥 Try to learn the patterns on your own.

If you would rather take a short cut, just go to my web site for the additional patterns.

💥 **AVOID** letting your opponent set up one of the patterns on **YOU!**

Neuro Booster

In this exercise you will need a deck of cards.

Remove ONE of the cards from the deck without looking at it. After looking through the REST of the deck, you will know the exact card that you removed every time.

Here's how:

When you look through the rest of the deck, you are going to ADD UP all of the values of the remaining 51 cards IN A VERY UNIQUE WAY!

All of the TENS, JACKS, QUEENS and KINGS, are going to equal "0"

All of the ACES are going to equal "1'

All other numbered cards are going to equal FACE value:

$$(2's = 2, \ 3's = 3, \ 4's = 4\ldots etc)$$

You are also going to maintain a SINGLE DIGIT COUNT while Ignoring the SUIT OF THE CARD!

EXAMPLE:

If the first "five" cards are (7, 5, 3, 2, 2). The total is "19", but your SINGLE DIGIT count total would be "9".
(Only use the last DIGIT, in this case it's a "9")

If the next card is a KING, JACK, QUEEN or TEN, the count would STILL be "9" because ALL "TEN" CARDS are equal to "0".

If the next card is a "4", your count would total "3", NOT 13. (9 + 4 = 1<u>3</u>)

You will continue this SINGLE DIGIT count until you get to the very last card.

When you finally get to the 51st card, the very last card in the deck, whatever the single digit count is, you are going to subtract that amount from "10", and the difference will be equal to the original card that was removed.

EXAMPLES:

If your single digit total at the end was "3" then subtracting 3 from 10 would equal "7"
Meaning that the original removed FACE DOWN card was a SEVEN.

(Once again, we are not concerning ourselves with the SUIT of the card)

If your single digit total "5" then subtracting 5 from 10 would equal "5"

If your single digit total was "0" then subtracting 0 from 10 would equal "10" with the original card removed being a TEN card. Meaning it was either a 10, Jack, Queen or King.

EXERCISE:

Try doing this at least once every day. Your goal is to do it in under a minute while correctly guessing the card that was removed.

THIS EXERCISE WILL NOT ONLY BOOST YOUR
FOCUS, MEMORY, AND SELF ESTEEM,

IT WILL ALSO STIMULATE **NEUROGENESIS** AND
NEUROPLASTICITY!

PokerMental

After shuffling a deck of cards, count off exactly 25 cards from the deck. Now try to form FIVE "PAT" HANDS using only the 25 cards.

A "PAT" hand is a FULL HOUSE, a FLUSH or a STRAIT.

A **FULL HOUSE** is a hand that contains three cards of one rank and two cards of another rank, such as 3♣ 3♠ 3♦ 6♣ 6♥.

A **FLUSH** is a hand that contains five cards all of the SAME SUIT, not all of sequential rank, such as K♣ 10♣ 7♣ 6♣ 4♣ .

A **STRAIT** is a hand that contains five cards of sequential rank, not all of the same suit, such as 7♣ 6♠ 5♠ 4♥ 3♥.

Exercise:

Deal yourself 25 cards and try to make 5 "PAT" poker hands.

Example:

Let's say the 25 cards dealt were:

J♦, 2♣, 3♣, Q♦, 9♥

9♠, 7♥, 8♠, Q♣, 3♦

4♦, A♣, 3♠, 10♥, 10♣

J♥, A♠, 2♦, 4♣, K♦

K♠, 2♥, 9♦, J♠, 7♠

Your **FIVE PAT HANDS** could be:

Hand 1 - Ace High Straight
A♠, K♠, Q♦, J♦, 10♣

Hand 2 - Club Flush
A♣, 2♣, 3♣, 4♣, Q♣

Hand 3 - Heart Flush
2♥, 7♥, 9♥, 10♥, J♥

Hand 4 - Diamond Flush
2♦, 3♦, 4♦, 9♦, K♦

Hand 5 - Spade Flush
3♠, 7♠, 8♠, 9♠, J♠

PokerMental is a great **TEAM EXERCISE** as well, and helps enhance **FOCUS AND THOUGHT.**

CALENDAR CODE

The Secret Formula to Knowing the Day of the Week for ANY DATE in 2025…

Someone gives you ANY DATE in the year 2025 and you will INSTANTLY know the day of the week that the date falls on.

The first thing you will have to do is learn a couple of codes.

A code for the MONTH and a code for the DATE.

Afterwards you just add the codes up and divide by "7" (the number of days in a week)

After dividing by "7", you are going to only concern yourself with the remainder.

Finally, whatever the remainder is, you ADD "2" to the total,

(2 is the YEAR CODE for 2025)

Now you're ready to compute the day of the week by referring to the day of the week chart.

This may seem complicated, but after doing it a few times it will become easy to do.

MONTH CODE:

January = 0	May = 1	September = 5
February = 3	June = 4	October = 0
March = 3	July = 6	November = 3
April = 6	August = 2	December = 5

DATE CODE:

The DATE and the CODE are exactly the same…

The 1st = 1

The 2nd = 2

The 3rd = 3

The 4th = 4, etc.

(all the way up to the 31st = 31)

Once again, to determine the day of the week, just add the codes for the month, with the date, then divide by 7.

EXAMPLE:

March 8th would be:

March = 3

8th = 8

3 + 8 = 11

11 ÷ 7 = 1 with a remainder of 4

💥You only concern yourself with the REMAINDER, which in this case is 4.

💥The final thing you do is ADD 2 (year code) from the total

4 + 2 = 6

When you have the final total, refer to the day of the week chart below. "6" would be a Saturday

 1 = Monday
 2 = Tuesday
 3 = Wednesday
 4 = Thursday
 5 = Friday
 6 = Saturday
 0 = Sunday

HERE ARE SOME MORE EXAMPLES:

FEBRUARY 14TH	OCTOBER 8TH	DECEMBER 25TH
February = 3	October = 0	December = 5
14th = 14	8th = 8	25th = 25
3 + 14 = 17	0 + 8 = 8	5 + 25 = 30
17 ÷ 7 = 2 (Remainder of 3)	8 ÷ 7 = 1 (Remainder of 1)	30 ÷ 7 = 4 (Remainder of 2)
3 + 2 **(year code)** = 5	1 + 2 = 3	2 + 2 = 4
5 = Friday	**3 = Wednesday**	**4 = Thursday**

If you would like to learn how to compute the date for **ANY YEAR**, all the way back to **1AD**, please go to: www.jimkarol.com

Chapter Two

Memory

The Memory exercises and demonstrations in this book are designed to help improve short-term memory, working memory, and long-term memory. The exercises emphasize verbal and visual mnemonics and associations that are powerful tools and easy to learn.

Memorizing NEW information stimulates Neurogenesis (the birth of new neurons) an Neuroplasticity (new connections)

Here are 3 of my favorite Building Blocks to enhance Memory:

Red Black Routine

Visual Link System

Mental Matrix

Red Black Routine

Remove 12 cards from a deck of cards. Try to remember all 12 colors. This is almost impossible unless you use a shortcut.

The Shortcut

Look at the top three cards
and focus on just the color RED

Example:

Top Card (T) 9♦

Middle Card (M) J♠

Bottom Card (B) 7♠

The 9 of diamonds is on top and is the ONLY red card in the group of three.

The **RED** is on **TOP**, so just remember "**T**" for **TOP**!

The next three cards are the Q♥ 7♦ 8♥

They are all red, so you would remember "**A**" for **ALL**

If the top two cards are black and the red card is on the bottom of the group of 3, you would remember "**B**" for **BOTTOM**.

Do the same with the next group of 3 focusing on just the color **RED** while referring to the chart of the eight possible outcomes on the next page

RED BLACK SYSTEM

EXAMPLE:

THERE ARE EIGHT POSSIBLE OUTCOMES.

RRR = A (All)
(All 3 cards are red)

RBB = T (Top)
(The Top card is red)

BBR = B (Bottom)
(Bottom card is red)

BRB = M (Middle)
(Middle card is red)

BBB = N (None)
(No cards are red)

RRB = U (Upper)
(Upper 2 cards are red)

BRR = L (Lower)
(Lower 2 cards are red)

RBR = O (Outer)
(Two Red outer cards)

If you can remember the letters **T - A - M - B**
you will easily remember the first 12 colors

VISUAL LINK SYSTEM

14 Words

1. CAR
2. CINDER BLOCK
3. BEAR
4. TOE
5. POTATOE
6. SWIMMING POOL
7. TAXICAB
8. PRIEST
9. SPAGHETTI
10. PING POIG BALLS
11. BUTTERFLY
12. COKE CAN
13. TABLE
14. TRIANGLE

To easily remember the **14 words**, all you need to do is <u>LINK</u> the **14 words** with a story. The more outrageous the story, the more likely you will remember it!

(IT IS VERY IMPORTANT TO TRY AND VISUALIZE AS YOU READ THE STORY)

Example Story:

"I was backing my **CAR** out of the driveway when, all of a sudden, I hit a **CINDER BLOCK**. I got out of my car and was amazed to see that the cinder block fell onto a **BEAR'S** big **TOE**. The angry bear was eating a **POTATO** and threw it at me, sailing into my neighbors **SWIMMING POOL**. When I walked towards the pool, I noticed that there wasn't any water in it, but there was a **TAXICAB** in the bottom of the pool. As I looked closer, I could see a **PRIEST** sitting in the back seat of the cab, and he was eating **SPAGHETTI**. He wasn't eating spaghetti and meatballs though; he was eating spaghetti and **PING PONG BALLS**. He stuck his head out the back window and had a ping pong ball in his opened mouth. When he spit it out, it turned into a beautiful **BUTTERFLY**. The butterfly flew onto a **COKE CAN** that was setting on an unusual looking glass **TABLE** which was shaped like a **TRIANGLE**!"

Most people hear this story ONE TIME and instantly remember ALL 14 WORDS!

The KEY, once again, is to visualize everything happening in your story.

EXERCISE:

LETS SEE IF YOU CAN REMEMBER THE 14 WORDS…

I was backing my _____ out of the driveway.

All of a sudden, I hit a _____ .

What did the cinder block fall on?

What was the bear eating?

Where did the potato end up?

What was in the bottom of the pool?

Who was in the back seat of the taxi?

What was the priest eating?

What did the priest spit out of his mouth when he put his head out the window?

What did the ping pong ball turn into?

Where did it land?

Great Job!
I'm sure that you got most, if not ALL of them right…

EXERCISE:

Create a story using your own random 10 to 15 words.

Mental Matrix

Jim's Mental Matrix

What exactly IS the Mental Matrix? Imagine visiting the Library of Congress and trying to find a book amongst 40 million books WITHOUT an INDEX CATALOGUE? Your brain is like a SUPER GIANT LIBRARY, in fact it can store more than 100 TIMES that of the Library of Congress!

My Mental Matrix acts as a MEGA Indexer to MY BRAIN.

It STORES and ORGANIZES everything to the Mental Matrix, then EASILY, retrieves FACTS and INFORMATION when needed.

I will show you how to develop YOUR OWN

MINI MENTAL MATRIX.

Mini Mental Matrix

I developed an Anchor System using names of celebrities.

Example:

(To begin, you must first memorize these seven celebrity names)

Denzel Washington

Brad Pitt

Tom Cruise

George Foreman

Michael J. Fox

Chris Rock

Sylvester Stallone

Here's how I did it!

I associated the names to numbers, then I added a little memory tip.

ONE) Denzel Washington
(George Washington the **first** president of the United States)

TWO) Brad Pitt
(1st letter in Brad is a "B", there are 2 "T's in Pitt)

THREE) Tom Cruise
(3 letters in Tom, the letter C in Cruise is the 3rd letter of the alphabet)

FOUR) George Foreman
(Four/Foreman)

FIVE) Michael J. Fox
(Fox Five is a television station's name, and "F" Five)

SIX) Chris Rock
(Six. I remember getting hit in the head with a rock when I was six. Personal stories make great memory tips)

SEVEN) Sylvester Stallone
(Sylvester, Stallone, and Seven. ALL 3 WORDS begin with the letter "S")

Once you have the 7 celebrities memorized, you will find it much easier to form additional lists as you develop your **OWN mini MENTAL MATRIX.**

7 STATES OF THE UNION

After memorizing the celebrities, I gave each celebrity a state. These are the actual FIRST SEVEN states of the union!

1) DELAWARE - Denzel Washington (Visualize DENZEL Washington crossing the Delaware)

2) PENNSYLVANIA - Brad PITT (PITT's burgh, PA)

3) NEW JERSEY - Tom CRUISE (CRUISING the JERSEY shore)

4) GEORGIA - GEORGE Foreman (GEORGE/Georgia)

5) CONNECTICUT - Michael J. FOX (the FOXwoods casino is located in Connecticut)

6) MASSACHUSETTS - Chris ROCK (Plymouth ROCK, Massachusetts)

7) MARYLAND - Sylvester Stallone (He always needed a doctor in his movies, MD for doctor and the initials for Maryland)

You now have the beginning of
YOUR OWN MENTAL MATRIX!

Add a playing card…

1. Denzel Washington
   (Ace of Diamonds (Denzel, Diamonds, Ace is first)
2. Brad Pitt
   (2 of Hearts (Brad Pitt is 2 and everybody loves him)
3. Tom Cruise
   (Jack of Clubs (Cruise, clubs and Jersey Jack)
4. George Foreman
   (King of Clubs (Foreman was the KING of CLUBBING boxers)
5. Michael J. Fox
   (4 of Hearts (Heart Foured, capital of Connecticut is Hartford)
6. Chris Rock
   (6 of Diamonds (Chris 6 and Rock is a diamond)
7. Sylvester Stallone
   (7 of Spades (Sylvester, Stallone, Seven Spades. All begin with an "S")

Now you have your own **MENTAL MATRIX**

7 long and 3 wide!

EXERCISE:

Practice reviewing the SEVEN Celebrities, States, and Playing Cards...

NOTE: The use of celebrities as anchors is the approach that is **USED BY ME**.

YOU can use people that relate to YOU as your anchors, such as family members and friends.

Chapter Three

Applications and More

This chapter is designed to improve powers of observation, deception detection and stress management. This component encourages participants to apply what they are learning to REAL-LIFE situations and challenges. These techniques will also help you remember names, stimulate creativity and boost self-esteem.

The three segments include:

Remembering Names

Flash Memory

ODD Skills

How to remember names

Not being able to remember someone's name, can be very embarrassing.

Attention and Focus are the KEY to remembering people's names.

Here are 3 important tips:

1. When meeting someone for the first time, REALLY PAY ATTENTION to their name and immediately repeat it OUT LOUD.
2. I sometimes even SPELL their name, out loud.
3. Try to associate their NAME to their FACE, or any specific features that might stand out.

💥If you FOCUS on just THESE THREE THINGS ALONE, it will GREATLY increase your chance of remembering their name.

If you aren't paying ATTENTION, your brain won't register their name in the first place, so you probably won't remember it. It is very important to REALLY LISTEN and don't be afraid to ask for their name again, especially if you didn't get it the first time.

I usually try to form a visual impression of the person. The more vividly you observe a person's physical appearance and characteristics, the more likely you will REMEMBER THEM.

Visualize their name to objects:

- Bill (dollar bill)
- John (toilet)
- Sue (lawyer)
- Dawn (sunrise)
- Jack (car)
- Allen (wrench)
- Mickey (mouse)
- Wendy (windy)
- Jim (Gym or SlimJim)
- Mike (microphone)

Ask for a Business Card

I always ask for a business card and say their name out loud as I'm reading it. REPEAT, REPEAT, REPEAT.
(repeat their name a few times when being introduced and during conversation)
When LEAVING, say their name AGAIN, one last time, "it was nice meeting you Mike" Repetition is the absolute KEY to memory. I usually put the more difficult names to MY MENTAL MATRIX.

FLASH MEMORY

Flash Memory is a technique that helps you sharpen and enhance Visual Perception, Focus and Memory at SUPER SPEED!

Instantly Recognize

- Objects
- License Plates
- Faces
- Playing Cards

FLASH MEMORY EXAMPLES:

Using the 7 previously memorized cards below, try to guess the missing card?

QUESTION: Which card is missing?

ANSWER: See next page

If you guessed the Two of Hearts, you were correct!

EXERCISE:

Place 5 objects on a table in front of you. Look at them for 10 seconds. Then turn your back.
Have someone remove one of the objects. You should instantly notice the missing object!

Begin with 5 objects and gradually work your way up to 10.

The more you practice Flash Memory, the faster you will become.

I can't say enough about how great this exercise is for you.

It dramatically improved my Focus and the more you practice the faster you get. It's absolutely amazing how much information you can receive with just a QUICK GLIMPSE…

ODD Skills

Observation and Deception Detection Skills

Observation Skills

The ability to observe and actively engage with your surroundings by focusing on details and actively paying attention to the present moment while using all your senses to take in information around you.

It is having the ability to ACCURATELY READ NONVERBAL clues that people give off.

Your ability to observe depends on how well you can get INTO THE ZONE…

"A mental state where someone is fully absorbed in an activity and experiences a high level of Focus, Concentration, Enjoyment, and Effortless Action."

Here are some great ways for enhancing your **Observation skills** that are covered in this book:

- **FLASH MEMORY TRAINING**
- **FOCUS EXERCISES**
- **MEMITATION**

Memorizing a deck of playing cards is MY personal favorite mental exercise that also helps me improve my observation skills.

Deception Detection Skills

The ability to determine TRUTH and INTEGRITY in a brief conversation. The first thing I usually do is establish a baseline. I usually do this by asking someone to say, "NO!" to any question I ask.

Tips to watch for deception AFTER asking a YES or NO question:

1. **FIDGETING**

2. **BLUSHING**

3. **LIP NIBBLING or PUCKERING**

4. **VOICE TONE has slight changes**

5. **BLINK PATTERN changes**
   (after being asked a question)

6. **PUPILS usually DILATE**
   (when the person is lying OR excited)

7. **EYES briefly look away**

8. **After saying "NO", they close their eyes**

9. **They slightly hesitate before saying "NO"**

10. **Slight HEAD movement**
    (sometimes actually nodding YES)

Chapter Four

Well-Being

The **Well-being** chapter emphasizes the relevance and importance of exercise, sleep hygiene, positivity, and healthy nutrition to complement and enhance the lessons about Focus, Attention and Memory.

I call the next two segments, ESPN and Memitation.

ESPN

E = EXERCISE

S = SLEEP

P = POSITIVITY

N = NUTRITION

E (EXERCISE)

We all know the benefits of PHYSICAL exercise. Here are the benefits of MENTAL exercise

- Enhanced cognitive abilities
- Slowing down the brain's aging process
- Increases brain mass.

S (SLEEP)

- A good night's sleep helps strengthen our immune system and ENERGIZES our BRAIN and BODY
- A good night's sleep has a positive effect on inflammation, stress and blood pressure
- A good night's sleep enables our glymphatic system to CLEAN UP OUR BRAIN and remove harmful toxins

P (POSITIVITY)

- Positive Thought boosts Confidence and Self-Esteem
- Positivity reduces STRESS
- Positivity helps to Stimulate CREATIVITY and a HEALTHY MIND!

N (NUTRITION)

- Good Nutrition STRENGTHENS our IMMUNE SYSTEM
- Good Nutrition reduces the risk of High Blood Pressure and Heart Disease
- Good nutrition Helps to BALANCE and ENHANCE most of our Neurotransmitters

MEMITATION

I came up with my own STRESS REDUCING formula, by combining cognitive fitness with meditation.

I call it MEMITATION.

Memitation is the act of reviewing memorized information in QUIET THOUGHT, while first focusing on BREATHING.

Focusing on my breathing and memory activity, clears my mind and enables me to achieve an emotionally calm state. Breathing properly is very important.

I usually Concentrate on breathing IN and OUT, deep from my gut, for about 3 minutes. Then I focus on POSITIVE THOUGHT or a positive experience in my life.

Soon after I begin to review something that I previously put to memory. This not only RELAXES me, but it also reduces STRESS and ANXIETY!

I once got out of a really bad, stressed-out mood, by just reviewing the 50 states while memitating for just 10 minutes.

After about 3 minutes of focusing on breathing, I review information that I've previously memorized, like the Countries and Capitals, the U.S. ZIP codes, Digits of Pi, etc. This can last anywhere from 5 mins to 10 mins. Afterwards, I really turn it up a notch and FOCUS INTENSELY on MYSELF and my SURROUNDINGS!

Memitation also helps me stay calm under pressure by creating an inner discipline!

The coolest thing of all is that it only takes 2 to 10 minutes and can be done ANYWHERE at ANY TIME.

Exercising my brain during memitation, enhances:

- **FOCUS**
- **CREATIVITY**
- **INTUITION**
- **KNOWLEDGE**
- **ENERGY**
- **SELF-ESTEEM**

I TRULY BELIEVE THAT **MEMITATION** AND **ESPN** ARE THE KEY TO BRAIN WELLNESS AND COGNITIVE FITNESS!

EXERCISE:

Try my Memitation technique using something that you've memorized from this book.

Chapter Five

Secret Math Codes

The information in this chapter is why I called this book **Mathematical Mind**.

From thousands of Barcode Numbers to 25 Random Decks, these are WITHOUT A DOUBT the most mysterious and extraordinary Mental Feats that I've ever come up with in my life.

EVERYTHING is 100% memorized and ALSO **Mathematically Connected.**

Clues on HOW YOU can crack the code are located throughout this book.

Anyone that cracks the code and are able to memorize the BARCODES and the 25 DECKS on the following pages, is an ABSOLUTE GENIUS!!!

Mathematical

Barcodes

4,392 Digits

001) 056675242213
002) 485331855149
003) 093318855650
004) 852943922913
005) 393815206542
006) 388998531819
007) 352792954250
008) 392293908944
009) 893153180944
010) 254166253118
011) 310041354755
012) 292235925325
013) 255418454931
014) 053814196588
015) 053381995399

016) 058408125201
017) 184524058394
018) 414454529057
019) 055659398535
020) 852580454985
021) 544953186852
022) 281469006978
023) 393815205841
024) 013149385295
025) 952259058901
026) 905254052586
027) 292231881578
028) 329405190355
029) 013195381411
030) 015254501390

031) 913152201319
032) 393815201319
033) 385253819521
034) 126139450857
035) 419094856631
036) 493521931753
037) 152943590458
038) 281353922994
039) 141391442580
040) 093122542918
041) 755875325545
042) 312175549470
043) 391535589119
044) 359255949659
045) 053352550545
046) 695835285941
047) 951435445850
048) 412944138524
049) 853184905849
050) 857996892294

051) 818899546584
052) 151418552590
053) 893818475856
054) 454652319894
055) 358714685531
056) 853150584954
057) 388990568583
058) 905251190941
059) 388990914921
060) 718599499516
061) 905254951712
062) 294495952089
063) 610893190531
064) 292253859012
065) 015358803990
066) 294352117842
067) 412942500583
068) 354145289540
069) 819952238535
070) 129353556583

071) 852580854658
072) 611245331408
073) 493145205488
074) 152942135465
075) 715409401814
076) 812185714453
077) 129197554199
078) 212192358056
079) 388995454452
080) 391505954817
081) 292275242587
082) 412941871500
083) 414151855422
084) 058475543140
085) 412943566586
086) 254909225835
087) 535439295441
088) 566559251845
089) 852580453455
090) 058859689475

091) 819829321178
092) 292258592258
093) 054905318001
094) 140549521445
095) 318854251005
096) 754581313149
097) 140854585619
098) 058445456638
099) 013595182054
100) 097583554908
101) 018199936181
102) 149312851954
103) 650450530925
104) 389451206985
105) 213105085610
106) 819885183889
107) 250812351654
108) 944565445435
109) 498054143947
110) 183175445425

111) 755439228140
112) 325955435140
113) 090149325541
114) 658859071360
115) 399995493659
116) 785195058408
117) 058394105818
118) 785329494144
119) 853512545055
120) 755465221985
121) 252582589229
122) 697803212281
123) 085410181239
124) 165375543540
125) 853159522590
126) 658899215225
127) 785902190589
128) 498058188532
129) 118105194013
130) 013905497809

131) 981609131522
132) 613556639381
133) 213109543852
134) 085754610858
135) 819431441909
136) 354198493521
137) 695245648513
138) 495818428135
139) 085310582551
140) 291829180931
141) 210314755875
142) 058853171985
143) 119094653589
144) 612669309543
145) 354942213105
146) 912947689210
147) 081529599514
148) 504129441385
149) 901831898531
150) 754539080853

151) 944914105459
152) 085310894151
153) 685005353148
154) 695385454652
155) 981398141854
156) 085853185315
157) 085455881405
158) 135893147816
159) 129543889909
160) 165225137185
161) 144589957590
162) 089625429449
163) 901808516108
164) 852547556085
165) 039905801535
166) 253552294352
167) 085545839904
168) 085396184565
169) 721491058819
170) 312257151293

171) 085909478525
172) 085819025861
173) 488518949314
174) 655025595152
175) 192229227154
176) 453514085658
177) 197554199075
178) 056714212192
179) 935405613531
180) 817947212239
181) 938944258929
182) 938513412941
183) 221592850858
184) 085629409054
185) 685453545441
186) 355008561854
187) 411595681661
188) 281258518056
189) 414359390835
190) 785900588596

191) 319122143181
192) 812253554292
193) 013119941325
194) 658851405495
195) 254495144325
196) 916583147545
197) 992543556085
198) 385352105613
199) 621450560851
200) 085785543925
201) 452131854525
202) 654495221491
203) 453058955085
204) 755879110214
205) 354453093108
206) 319913819500
207) 318521441441
208) 951083185294
209) 453813698985
210) 298794918938
211) 453558112214
212) 458083185294
213) 885459921446
214) 258354035406
215) 154013156814
216) 054459955419
217) 589535213219
218) 251999141210
219) 944914194491
220) 399999996690
221) 922945999689
222) 121213135407
223) 319451171901
224) 399951890566
225) 181149192900
226) 393897142149
227) 625894101221
228) 054191190940
229) 953145935945
230) 399354994314

231) 312965849191
232) 394459501919
233) 585754912530
234) 114919056511
235) 359029879491
236) 452141318954
237) 452819112943
238) 352581454542
239) 458084115012
240) 951084115016
241) 354014185254
242) 319894705452
243) 941852599500
244) 355394738555
245) 101891202115
246) 512185315121
247) 453354935914
248) 189654168554
249) 121911014511
250) 813199854521

251) 452584521318
252) 818899218765
253) 085405445305
254) 102140175587
255) 818065843544
256) 259054319913
257) 144165299318
258) 352132919510
259) 354358445381
260) 893835442987
261) 122145453558
262) 812597845808
263) 685294543588
264) 354065295825
265) 681416580154
266) 419829225054
267) 352132195895
268) 210548517525
269) 944914165299
270) 013195439999

271) 968947695249
272) 354075458512
273) 117190131945
274) 056658954390
275) 290025853118
276) 214994739389
277) 012218199556
278) 119094054190
279) 459359459953
280) 314995439935
281) 913813540531
282) 919406112394
283) 912535857540
284) 056511114919
285) 381825905435
286) 318954390545
287) 294352445281
288) 454258352581
289) 299318314580
290) 695885951084

291) 852541354014
292) 525369131989
293) 259959418500
294) 385554453553
295) 912021153905
296) 512185313905
297) 914016545335
298) 685549418965
299) 014511121911
300) 854521218131
301) 085259035824
302) 318895485331
303) 413214441325
304) 755435849472
305) 085135893146
306) 518087111538
307) 997493527929
308) 913257544392
309) 085498054565
310) 254818254166

311) 085456180543
312) 194715472922
313) 659594541425
314) 055905850538
315) 318560853582
316) 819896815058
317) 094725122085
318) 014948925841
319) 319945055659
320) 085614852580
321) 353947051358
322) 941038281469
323) 219150212249
324) 545625352580
325) 813259522590
326) 085405518524
327) 938557542922
328) 085755408521
329) 540580854817
330) 988510152545

331) 941159541621
332) 497805608529
333) 388990319213
334) 931861351261
335) 125110961239
336) 145394749352
337) 085140513812
338) 085994089549
339) 085254759051
340) 392485790931
341) 085418114978
342) 354568545831
343) 315459358243
344) 389053543140
345) 354942213120
346) 053588534525
347) 085694161408
348) 112965849141
349) 689210561809
350) 416541443546

351) 085617909258
352) 085415085518
353) 135893142511
354) 853532580850
355) 587543587146
356) 985431485315
357) 210314850184
358) 085385902589

359) 318910013193
360) 121449471859
361) 121478535490
362) 085619014408
363) 901808117545
364) 221694791442
365) 615906583184
366) 685432119294

25 Random Decks

ALL 25 decks, which include a total of 1300 cards, are completely memorized.
All 25 decks are mathematically connected.
Clues on HOW YOU can crack the code are located throughout this book.
**Once again, anyone that is able to memorize the 25 decks, is an
ABSOLUTE GENIUS!**

NOTE:

The next several pages provide you with each of the 25 decks that I've remembered.

You're welcome to buy 25 decks of cards, then mark or identify them with your own titles and use actual decks of playing cards to remember.

Okay, here we go.
The next page has the first deck of 25 decks laid out in the precise order of my actual **M1**- deck.

Focus
and
Start memorizing

M1
Deck

1) Q♡
2) 3♠
3) 4♠
4) K♡
5) 10♢
6) 10♣
7) 8♢
8) 9♣
9) K♠
10) 4♡
11) 5♡
12) 2♠
13) 4♣
14) J♢
15) J♠
16) Q♢
17) 2♣
18) 3♡
19) 5♠
20) A♡
21) A♣
22) 3♢
23) 10♡
24) Q♣
25) 8♣
26) K♢
27) 8♡
28) 9♢
29) Q♠
30) A♢
31) 7♣
32) K♣
33) 9♠
34) 2♡
35) 6♢
36) 10♠
37) 8♠
38) 3♣
39) 2♢
40) J♡
41) 6♠
42) 6♣
43) 4♢
44) 5♣
45) J♣
46) 7♢
47) 7♠
48) 9♡
49) A♠
50) 6♡
51) 5♢
52) 7♡

M2 DECK

1) 2♡
2) 3♢
3) Q♠
4) A♠
5) 5♢
6) 7♡
7) 8♣
8) 8♠
9) 10♢
10) 6♡
11) 2♢
12) 10♠
13) 4♣
14) 6♣
15) A♢
16) J♣
17) K♠
18) 9♡
19) 6♢
20) Q♣
21) 2♠
22) 3♠
23) 10♡
24) 5♣
25) 3♡
26) 7♢
27) 5♡
28) A♣
29) J♡
30) 4♢
31) 2♣
32) 8♢
33) 9♣
34) A♡
35) 6♠
36) Q♡
37) K♣
38) 9♠
39) 10♣
40) 8♡
41) J♢
42) J♠
43) 4♠
44) 5♠
45) K♡
46) 7♠
47) Q♢
48) 9♢
49) 4♡
50) K♢
51) 7♣
52) 3♣

MV DECK

1) A♠
2) 10♡
3) 9♡
4) K♠
5) 3♣
6) 3♢
7) 5♣
8) 4♢
9) K♡
10) 9♠
11) 8♠
12) J♡
13) 9♢
14) 2♣
15) 2♡
16) A♣
17) J♡
18) 10♠
19) 8♡
20) Q♠
21) Q♢
22) 10♣
23) 3♠
24) A♢
25) 5♢
26) K♣
27) 5♠
28) 4♣
29) A♡
30) Q♣
31) 6♢
32) K♢
33) 4♡
34) J♠
35) 7♣
36) 3♡
37) 5♡
38) 10♢
39) J♣
40) 2♠
41) 7♡
42) 7♢
43) 9♣
44) 8♢
45) 2♢
46) 6♣
47) 6♡
48) 4♠
49) Q♡
50) 7♠
51) 8♣
52) 6♠

MX Deck

1) 5♡
2) Q♣
3) 8♢
4) A♡
5) 4♠
6) K♡
7) 2♠
8) 8♣
9) 9♣
10) Q♢
11) 2♣
12) 10♢
13) 4♣
14) A♣
15) K♠
16) 4♡
17) 3♡
18) Q♡
19) J♢
20) 3♢
21) 10♡
22) 10♣
23) 5♠
24) 3♣
25) J♠
26) K♢
27) 7♣
28) 10♠
29) 6♠
30) 7♢
31) 5♢
32) Q♠
33) 2♡
34) 2♢
35) 5♣
36) A♠
37) 8♡
38) K♣
39) 8♠
40) 6♣
41) 7♠
42) 7♡
43) A♢
44) 6♢
45) J♡
46) J♣
47) 6♡
48) 9♢
49) 9♠
50) 3♣
51) 4♢
52) 9♡

Q Deck

1) J♢
2) 2♣
3) 3♣
4) Q♢
5) 9♡
6) 9♣
7) 7♡
8) 8♠
9) Q♣
10) 3♢
11) 4♢
12) A♣
13) 3♠
14) 10♡
15) 10♣
16) J♡
17) A♠
18) 2♢
19) 4♣
20) K♢
21) K♠
22) 2♡
23) 9♢
24) J♠
25) 7♠
26) Q♡
27) 7♢
28) 8♡
29) J♣
30) K♡
31) 6♠
32) Q♠
33) 8♣
34) A♢
35) 5♢
36) 9♣
37) 7♣
38) 2♠
39) A♡
40) 10♢
41) 5♣
42) 5♡
43) 3♡
44) 4♠
45) 10♠
46) 6♡
47) 6♣
48) 8♢
49) K♣
50) 5♢
51) 4♡
52) 6♢

Qi Deck

1) J♦
2) 10♥
3) 7♦
4) 10♦
5) 2♣
6) 10♣
7) 8♥
8) 5♣
9) 3♣
10) J♥
11) J♣
12) 5♠
13) Q♦
14) A♠
15) K♥
16) 3♥
17) 9♥
18) 2♦
19) 6♠
20) 4♠
21) 9♠
22) 4♣
23) Q♠
24) 10♠
25) 7♥
26) K♦
27) 8♣
28) 6♥
29) 8♠
30) K♠
31) A♦
32) 6♣
33) Q♣
34) 2♥
35) 5♥
36) 8♦
37) 3♦
38) 9♦
39) 9♣
40) K♣
41) 4♦
42) J♠
43) 7♣
44) 5♦
45) A♣
46) 7♠
47) 2♠
48) 4♥
49) 3♠
50) Q♥
51) A♥
52) 6♦

V Deck

1) 2♣
2) J♦
3) 10♦
4) A♣
5) 4♠
6) 4♥
7) 6♠
8) 5♥
9) A♦
10) 10♣
11) 9♣
12) Q♦
13) 10♥
14) 3♠
15) 3♥
16) 2♠
17) Q♥
18) J♣
19) 9♦
20) K♣
21) K♥
22) J♠
23) 4♣
24) 2♥
25) 6♥
26) A♠
27) 6♣
28) 5♠
29) 2♦
30) K♠
31) 7♥
32) A♥
33) 5♦
34) Q♣
35) 8♠
36) 4♦
37) 6♦
38) J♥
39) Q♠
40) 3♣
41) 8♠
42) 8♥
43) 10♦
44) 9♥
45) 3♦
46) 7♠
47) 7♦
48) 5♣
49) K♦
50) 8♣
51) 9♠
52) 7♣

T Deck

1) J♢
2) 4♢
3) K♠
4) 6♠
5) 5♣
6) 2♣
7) A♣
8) 2♡
9) Q♠
10) 5♠
11) 3♣
12) 3♠
13) 9♢
14) 8♣
15) 3♡
16) Q♢
17) 10♡
18) J♠
19) A♢
20) 4♠
21) 9♡
22) 10♣
23) 7♠
24) 5♡
25) 10♠
26) 9♠
27) J♡
38) Q♡
29) 9♣
30) 6♡
31) 7♡
32) A♠
33) 7♢
34) 7♣
35) 6♣
36) 8♠
37) 2♢
38) 8♡
39) 2♠
40) 8♢
41) Q♣
42) 4♣
43) J♣
44) A♡
45) K♣
46) 3♢
47) K♢
48) K♡
49) 10♢
50) 5♢
51) 4♡
52) 6♢

US Deck

1) A♢
2) 2♡
3) J♣
4) K♣
5) 4♢
6) 6♢
7) 7♠
8) 7♣
9) 9♡
10) 5♢
11) A♡
12) 9♣
13) 3♠
14) 5♠
15) K♡
16) 10♠
17) Q♣
18) 8♢
19) 5♡
20) J♠
21) A♣
22) 2♣
23) 9♢
24) 4♠
25) 2♢
26) 6♡
27) 4♢
28) K♠
29) 10♢
30) 3♡
31) A♠
32) 7♡
33) 8♠
34) K♢
35) 5♣
36) J♢
37) Q♠
38) 8♣
39) 9♠
40) 7♢
41) 10♡
42) 10♣
43) 3♣
44) 4♣
45) Q♢
46) 6♣
47) J♡
48) 8♡
49) 3♢
50) Q♡
51) 6♠
52) 2♠

X3 DECK

1) Q♦
2) Q♣
3) 2♣
4) 3♣
5) 9♥
6) 7♥
7) 8♠
8) J♦
9) 9♠
10) 3♦
11) 10♥
12) 4♣
13) A♣
14) 3♠
15) 10♣
16) A♠
17) 2♦
18) 4♦
19) J♥
20) K♦
21) J♠
22) J♣
23) 2♥
24) 9♦
25) 7♠
26) 7♦
27) 8♥
28) K♠
29) Q♥
30) K♥
31) A♦
32) A♥
33) Q♠
34) 8♣
35) 5♥
36) 7♣
37) 2♠
38) 6♠
39) 9♣
40) 10♦
41) 4♠
42) K♣
43) 5♠
44) 3♥
45) 10♠
46) 6♣
47) 8♦
48) 5♣
49) 6♥
50) 5♦
51) 4♥
52) 6♦

X4 DECK

1) 8♠
2) 4♦
3) 10♥
4) J♦
5) 3♠
6) 2♣
7) 7♥
8) A♣
9) 3♣
10) J♥
11) Q♣
12) 9♠
13) 3♦
14) 9♥
15) Q♦
16) 10♣
17) A♠
18) K♠
19) 7♠
20) K♦
21) J♠
22) 4♣
23) 9♦
24) 2♦
25) 2♥
26) Q♥
27) K♥
28) A♦
29) 2♠
30) 5♠
31) 6♥
32) 5♦
33) 7♦
34) 6♠
35) 5♥
36) A♥
37) 3♥
38) 6♣
39) 4♥
40) 8♥
41) Q♠
42) 9♣
43) 10♦
44) 4♠
45) 8♦
46) 6♦
47) J♣
48) 8♣
49) 7♣
50) 5♣
51) 10♠
52) K♣

X5
Deck

1) 4♢
2) J♠
3) 7♡
4) K♢
5) 3♣
6) Q♢
7) A♣
8) 7♠
9) 8♠
10) J♡
11) A♠
12) 9♡
13) 3♠
14) K♠
15) Q♣
16) 3♢
17) 2♢
18) J♠
19) 10♡
20) 2♡
21) 9♢
22) 9♠
23) 4♣
24) 2♣
25) 10♣
26) Q♡
27) 6♠
28) 9
29) 5♣
30) 6♡
31) 4♡
32) J♣
33) A♢
34) A♡
35) 4♠
36) K♣
37) 7♢
38) Q♠
39) 7♣
40) 5♠
41) 6♣
42) 6♢
43) K♡
44) 5♡
45) 10♢
46) 10♠
47) 5♢
48) 8♡
49) 8♣
50) 2♠
51) 3♡
52) 8♢

X6.7
Deck

1) 9♠
2) Q♠
3) 3♣
4) A♢
5) 5♡
6) J♡
7) 7♡
8) 4♢
9) 7♢
10) 8♡
11) 8♠
12) K♡
13) 4♣
14) 10♡
15) J♡
16) 10♣
17) 9♢
18) J♠
19) 2♢
20) K♢
21) 2♡
22) K♠
23) A♠
24) 3♠
25) 7♠
26) J♣
27) 3♢
28) Q♣
29) Q♡
30) A♣
31) 9♣
32) 9♡
33) 8♣
34) Q♢
35) 2♣
36) 6♠
37) 7♣
38) 4♠
39) 4♡
40) 5♠
41) K♣
42) 10♢
43) 6♣
44) 2♠
45) 10♠
46) 6♢
47) 3♡
48) 5♢
49) 5♣
50) 8♢
51) A♡
52) 6♡

X7 DECK

1) 2♥
2) 6♣
3) J♥
4) 5♣
5) 3♦
6) 5♥
7) Q♦
8) 9♥
9) 9♣
10) 8♦
11) A♠
12) 5♠
13) 4♦
14) J♣
15) K♥
16) 9♠
17) J♠
18) K♣
19) 2♦
20) 9♣
21) A♣
22) 3♠
23) 6♠
24) 7♥
25) 7♠
26) 3♥
27) 4♣
28) 7♣
29) 2♠
30) 10♥
31) Q♠
32) J♠
33) Q♥
35) 4♠
35) K♦
36) K♠
37) A♥
38) 8♠
39) 8♣
40) 2♣
41) 7♦
42) 10♠
43) 6♥
44) 10♣
45) 10♦
46) Q♣
47) A♦
48) 3♣
49) 8♥
50) 5♦
51) 4♥
52) 6♦

Q3 DECK

1) 3♣
2) 9♠
3) Q♣
4) A♣
5) 10♣
6) 2♦
7) K♠
8) J♠
9) 7♦
10) K♥
11) 8♣
12) 9♣
13) A♥
14) 5♠
15) 10♠
16) 8♦
17) 4♥
18) 2♣
19) 9♥
20) 8♠
21) 4♥
22) 10♥
23) A♠
24) K♦
25) 9♦
26) Q♥
27) J♣
28) Q♠
29) 5♥
30) 2♠
31) 5♣
32) 4♠
33) 6♣
34) 5♦
35) J♦
36) Q♦
37) 7♥
38) 3♦
39) 3♠
40) J♥
41) 4♣
42) 2♥
43) 7♠
44) 8♥
45) 6♠
46) A♦
47) 7♣
48) 10♦
49) 3♥
50) 6♥
51) K♣
52) 6♦

XV Deck

1) 9♣
2) 2♡
3) 6♠
4) K♣
5) 10♢
6) A♣
7) Q♢
8) 6♡
9) 5♡
10) 2♠
11) Q♡
12) 4♠
13) 10♡
14) K♡
15) A♢
16) 10♣
17) J♣
18) 2♣
19) 3♠
20) J♠
21) 4♣
22) 4♡
23) 9♢
24) J♢
25) 3♢
26) A♠
27) 7♡
28) 4♢
29) 8♢
30) 7♠
31) 9♠
32) 2♢
33) Q♣
34) Q♠
35) 9♡
36) K♢
37) 6♣
38) A♡
39) 6♢
40) 8♡
41) 7♢
42) 7♣
43) K♠
44) 8♠
45) 3♣
46) 3♡
47) 8♣
48) 5♠
49) 5♢
50) J♡
51) 10♠
52) 5♣

F1 Deck

1) J♢
2) 2♣
3) 3♣
4) 4♠
5) 9♡
6) Q♢
7) 10♡
8) 4♣
9) 9♠
10) 3♡
11) J♣
12) 10♣
13) 7♢
14) 10♠
15) 8♡
16) J♡
17) 2♢
18) 5♣
19) 5♠
20) K♡
21) Q♠
22) 10♢
23) 6♠
24) A♠
25) 7♡
26) Q♡
27) 7♠
28) 8♢
29) Q♣
30) K♠
31) 5♡
32) 2♠
33) 3♢
34) A♣
35) 9♣
36) 6♡
37) 3♠
38) 5♢
39) 6♣
40) K♢
41) A♡
42) 8♠
43) 4♢
44) 8♣
45) 9♢
46) 2♡
47) J♠
48) A♢
49) 7♣
50) K♣
51) 4♡
52) 6♢

M3 Deck

1) K♡
2) K♠
3) 3♠
4) 4♠
5) 10♢
6) 8♢
7) 9♣
8) Q♡
9) 10♣
10) 4♡
11) J♢
12) 5♠
13) 2♠
14) 4♣
15) J♠
16) 2♣
17) 3♡
18) 5♢
19) Q♢
20) A♡
21) Q♣
22) Q♠
23) 3♢
24) 10♡
25) 8♣
26) 8♡
27) 9♢
28) A♣
29) K♢
30) A♢
31) 2♡
32) 2♢
33) K♣
34) 9
35) 6♢
36) 8♠
37) 3♣
38) 7♣
39) 10♠
40) J♡
41) 5♣
42) A♠
43) 6♣
44) 4♢
45) J♣
46) 7♠
47) 9♡
48) 6♠
49) 7♢
50) 6♡
51) 5♢
52) 7♡

V3 Deck

1) 10♢
2) 4♡
3) A♢
4) Q♢
5) 3♢
6) J♣
7) K♡
8) 2♡
9) 6♣
10) K♠
11) 5♢
12) 4♢
13) Q♠
14) 8♡
15) 3♡
16) 5♣
17) 9♠
18) J♢
19) 4♠
20) 5♡
21) 9♣
22) 3♠
23) Q♡
24) K♣
25) 4♣
26) A♠
27) 2♢
28) A♡
29) 8♠
30) J♡
31) 8♢
32) 9♡
33) 7♢
34) 8♣
35) 2♣
36) A♣
37) 6♠
38) 10♣
39) 10♡
40) 2♠
41) 9♢
42) J♠
43) 6♡
44) 5♠
45) 7♡
46) Q♣
47) 6♢
48) 3♣
49) 10♠
50) 7♠
51) K♢
52) 7♣

M4 DECK

1) 9♣
2) 5♥
3) J◇
4) Q♥
5) 4♣
6) 3♠
7) 8◇
8) 2♠
9) 4♠
10) Q◇
11) K♠
12) 10♣
13) 4♥
14) 10◇
15) K♥
16) J♠
17) 2♣
18) A♣
19) 8♣
20) A♥
21) Q♣
22) 5♠
23) 10♥
24) 3♥
25) 3◇
26) K◇
27) A◇
28) 2♥
29) 3♣
30) 6♣
31) 7◇
32) 6♥
33) 8♥
34) 7♣
35) 6◇
36) 2◇
37) 4◇
38) 7♠
39) 5◇
40) 9◇
41) K♣
42) 10♠
43) J♥
44) 5♣
45) 9♥
46) 7♥
47) Q♠
48) 9♠
49) 8♠
50) 6♠
51) J♣
52) A♠

Q7 DECK

1) 7♥
2) 10♥
3) K♠
4) 8♥
5) 5♥
6) 5♠
7) K♣
8) Q◇
9) 4◇
10) 2◇
11) 7♠
12) Q♠
13) A♥
14) 6♥
15) J◇
16) 8♠
17) 10♣
18) 2♥
19) J♣
20) 9♣
21) 3♥
22) 5◇
23) 9♥
24) A♣
25) 4♣
26) Q♥
27) 8♣
28) 10◇
29) 6♣
30) 2♣
31) Q♣
32) J♥
33) 9◇
34) K♥
35) 7♣
36) 4♠
37) 4
38) 9♠
39) 3♠
40) K◇
41) 7◇
42) A◇
43) 5♣
44) 8◇
45) 3♣
46) 3◇
47) A♠
48) J♠
49) 6♠
50) 2♠
51) 10♠
52) 6◇

USV DECK

1) Q♣
2) J♠
3) 2♦
4) K♦
5) 9♠
6) 7♣
7) 6♥
8) 6♦
9) 4♠
10) 8♣
11) Q♠
12) 4♦
13) 10♥
14) 8♥
15) K♠
16) 3♥
17) A♦
18) 5♣
19) 8♠
20) 2♥
21) Q♦
22) J♦
23) 4♣
24) 9♥
25) J♣
26) 7♠
27) 9♣
28) K♥
29) 3♣
30) 10♠
31) Q♥
32) 6♠
33) 5
34) K♣
35) 8♦
36) 2♣
37) A♥
38) 5♦
39) 4♥
40) 6♣
41) 3♠
42) 3♦
43) 10♦
44) 9♦
45) A♣
46) 7♦
47) 2♠
48) 5♠
49) 10♣
50) A♠
51) 7♥
52) J♥

US3 DECK

1) J♣
2) 6♦
3) 9♥
4) 9♣
5) K♥
6) 8♦
7) A♣
8) 4♠
9) 4♦
10) 3♥
11) 8♠
12) J
13) 9♠
14) 10♣
15) Q♦
16) 8♥
17) 6♠
18) 2♥
19) 4♥
20) 7♣
21) A♥
22) 5♥
23) Q♣
24) J♠
25) 9♦
26) 6♥
27) 10♦
28) 7♥
29) 5♣
30) 8♠
31) 10♥
32) 4♣
33) J♥
34) Q♥
35) A♦
36) K♣
37) 7♠
38) 5♦
39) 3♦
40) 10♠
41) 5♥
42) 2♣
43) 2♦
44) K♠
45) A♠
46) K♦
47) Q♠
48) 7♦
49) 3♣
50) 6♣
51) 3♦
52) 2♠

Q5 DECK

1) 9♡
2) 3♢
3) 10♣
4) K♢
5) 7♠
6) K♡
7) 5♡
8) 10♢
9) 10♠
10) 5♢
11) 3♣
12) 8♠
13) 3♠
14) 2♢
15) 9♢
16) 8♡
17) 8♣
18) 2♠
19) 3♡
20) 8♢
21) J♢
22) 9♠
23) 4♢
24) J♡
25) K
26) Q♡
27) 6♠
28) 9♣
29) 5♣
30) 6♡
31) 4♡
32) Q♢
33) Q♣
34) 10♡
35) 4♣
36) J♠
37) J♣
38) A♢
39) A♡
40) 4♠
41) K♣
42) 2♣
43) 7♡
44) A♣
45) A♠
46) 2♡
47) 7♢
48) Q♠
49) 7♣
50) 5♠
51) 6♣
52) 6♢

VZ DECK

1) 2♣
2) 1♢
3) 4♠
4) 6♠
5) A♢
6) 9♣
7) 10♡
8) 3♢
9) Q♡
10) 9♢
11) K♡
12) 4♣
13) 6♡
14) J♢
15) A♣
16) 4♡
17) 5♡
18) 10♣
19) Q♢
20) 3♠
21) 2♠
22) J♣
23) K♣
24) J♠
25) 2♡
26) A♠
27) 5♠
28) K♠
29) A♡
30) Q♣
31) 4♢
32) J♡
33) 3♣
34) 8♡
35) 9♡
36) 7♠
37) 5♣
38) 8♣
39) 7♣
40) 6♣
41) 2♢
42) 7♡
43) 5♢
44) 8♠
45) 6♢
46) Q♠
47) 8♢
48) 10♠
49) 3♡
50) 7♢
51) K♢
52) 9♠

There you have it!
This is a very small sample of what the mind is capable of. If you would like to learn more, about how to memorize playing cards, please visit my website at: www.jimkarol.com

ONE MORE THING

Socializing

Socializing is also a great way to boost your brain power. Here are some of my favorites…

- Don't just sit at home alone. Find a friend or family member and go to the movies, go to a play, visit a museum, start a book club; etc.
- Take a class at a local college.
- Learn how to play an instrument and practice playing music with others.
- Participate in a neighborhood or community group.
- Start a GAME NIGHT and play cards or board games with others.
- Exercise with a friend by walking, jogging, or going to the gym together.
- Play a group sport like bowling, golf, or croquet.
- My wife Lynn and I love when our grandkids visit. We have a lot of fun playing Memory and brain-boosting games, like Clue and Scrabble
- Get a PUPPY…

Most Important of All, HAVE FUN…

Thank you for taking action towards a healthier brain and a healthier you.

I welcome you to visit my website www.jimkarol.com where you can get more information about my **Cogmental Intelligence Program**.

About Jim Karol

Jim Karol is a world-renowned mentalist, memory expert, and motivational speaker whose unparalleled cognitive abilities have captivated millions. He is the author of ***Ultimate Memory Magic***, a groundbreaking book on harnessing memory for peak performance, health, and confidence. From network television and USO tours to top universities and Fortune 500 boardrooms, Jim uses his talents to entertain, educate, and empower people around the globe. His mission: to unlock the hidden potential of the human mind-one unforgettable moment at a time.

Learn more at: www.jimkarol.com

-Bonus Page-

*FOR ALL YOU POKER LOVERS
THE NEXT TIME YOU WANT TO HAVE FUN
WITH YOUR FRIENDS*

Look like a poker pro-

Offer to show your friends a new kind of poker game. Explain that it is played with 10 cards: 3 tens, 3 Queens, 3 Kings and a Jack of hearts. Have someone shuffle the cards and spread them out on the table face down. You and a friend take turns picking a card for your hand. When all ten cards are chosen each of you turns them face up and highest poker hand wins. You play this game a couple of times and you win some and you lose some. But as soon as a bet is made, you win every time.

(You will **ALWAYS** win whenever you want to)

How it's done-

The first thing you need to do is make a mark on the back of the Jack of hearts so that you can identify it when the cards are spread out face down. A pencil dot or a scratch works well. I like to put a RED dot right in the middle circle of a RED Bicycle card. Whatever you do, just don't make the mark too obvious. The key to winning the poker hand is to NOT pick the marked card, the Jack. Because no matter what other cards are chosen, whoever picks the Jack will ALWAYS lose. Make sure during the crucial betting hand that you pick first, so that there is no chance of being stuck with the Jack.

This jewel is worth the price of the book

I have been doing this routine for 50+ years
and have never had anyone figure it out!

www.ingramcontent.com/pod-product-compliance
Lightning Source LLC
Chambersburg PA
CBHW061751070526
44585CB00025B/2863